How to Begin
Writing
Your Life Stories

Also by Sara Roahen

*Gumbo Tales: Finding My Place
at the New Orleans Table*

*The Southern Foodways Alliance
Community Cookbook*
(co-editor)

This beginner's guide to life story writing is a prequel to a longer, more thorough, book on the same topic soon to be released by Demitasse Press. Visit www.sararoahen.com to sign up for updates on the longer book, for information on Sara's editing and coaching services, and for more life story writing ideas and resources.

How to Begin *Writing* Your Life Stories

Putting Memories on the Page

Sara Roahen

demitasse press
San Luis Obispo

Demitasse Press
San Luis Obispo, California

Print ISBN: 979-8-9903911-0-9
eBook ISBN: 979-8-9903911-1-6

Names: Roahen, Sara, author.
Title: How to begin writing your life stories : putting memories on the page / Sara Roahen.
Description: San Luis Obispo : Demitasse Press, [2024] | Includes bibliographical references and index.
Identifiers: ISBN: 979-8-9903911-0-9 (paperback) | 979-8-9903911-1-6 (ebook) | LCCN: 2024906259
Subjects: LCSH: Autobiography--Handbooks, manuals, etc. | Biography--Handbooks, manuals, etc. | Authorship--Handbooks, manuals, etc. | LCGFT: Reference works. | Handbooks and manuals. | BISAC: LANGUAGE ARTS & DISCIPLINES / Writing / Authorship. | BIOGRAPHY & AUTOBIOGRAPHY / Memoirs. | REFERENCE / Personal & Practical Guides.
Classification: LCC: CT85 .R63 2024 | DDC: 920/.0072--dc23

Book Design by Dorka Hegedus

For the inner storyteller in us all

"When you write your family history, be a recording angel and record everything your descendants might want to know."

William Zinsser, *On Writing Well*

Contents

Introduction

Congratulations on taking this first step to getting your memories on the page, to documenting the stories only you can tell.

I know a million other things want your attention. You're probably asking yourself, even right now as you read, *Do I really have time to write?* If I may offer an answer: That's a matter of perspective. Our days are wickedly short, and yet as long as we breathe, time remains our most reliable resource, our most faithful companion. Will you ever have enough time to accomplish everything on your list? Probably not. But you can choose how to arrange that list. And by picking up this primer you've chosen to at least consider putting writing your life stories near the top.

I'm so happy you're here!

For several years I've been teaching weekly life story writing classes to adults through my local community college. Some of my students have made beautiful story collections to present to their loved ones, some of my students have published—or will publish—memoirs, and some of my students write only for themselves. All reasons for writing the stories of our lives are valid and lead to reward. While it may sound like an expendable, narcissistic endeavor to people who have never done it, writing about ourselves and our lives is as beneficial to our health and well-being as are other more broadly endorsed acts of self-care, like eating healthfully and getting regular exercise.

Sounds implausible? James Pennebaker, a professor of psychology at the University of Texas at Austin, has studied the effects of what he calls "expressive writing" and determined that writing about our own lives (as in the style of journaling) is associated with improvements in physical health, improvements in markers of mental health, and improvements in immune function. Expressive writing has even been associated with improvements in working memory in college students. (See the Notes at the end of the book for more about Pennebaker's research.)

My students are beyond the age when people typically attend college, but they, too, consistently report that writing their stories coaxes memories to the surface they haven't thought about for decades—sometimes not since childhood. They also marvel at how writing about their past positively impacts their outlook on life today. My own spirit rests easier on days when I've transferred a life story from my head to the page. Sometimes the act of writing it down allows me to relive a good memory, and sometimes the process brings me to a new or deeper understanding of an emotionally complicated memory.

My hope is that this life story writing primer will inspire you to begin. To write that first sentence, record that first memory, and see how it feels. If my experience as writer and teacher is a reliable barometer, writing down the first story from your life will be the nudge you need to write the next. And the next. Soon enough you'll have a pile of stories. You know what I call a pile of life stories? A gift. One you may choose to share or keep for yourself.

The six prompts at the end of the guide are designed to help you begin. If you get stuck along the way and need motivation, or if you write on all the prompts and want more, please get in touch.

Yours in putting memories on the page,

Sara
hello@sararoahen.com

Life Story Writing

What are you doing here exactly? You've taken the plunge by opening this book. Maybe you've even written about a few of your memories. But you're still not exactly sure what to call what you're doing. And it bugs you. Are you writing a memoir? An autobiography? A personal history? A family history? Something else?

Here's the truth: It doesn't matter what you call it. You're writing, and if you keep at it you'll have more memories on the page than you ever imagined you could produce. When you spend more time defining what you're doing than writing, that's called procrastination, and procrastination leads to self-doubt, which is a creativity killer. If that sounds like a familiar pattern, the next time procrastination and self-doubt creep in, take a pause, politely inform them they weren't invited to your writing party, and remind yourself of the commitment you made. Maybe you've vowed to write one story a week for a year, or maybe your practice is writing for two hours every other Sunday morning after letting the dog out. Whatever your commitment to writing looks like, tattoo that to your mind's eye and take comfort in it. That commitment is real and precious and yours, and it will yield results.

Writing is writing. Deep breath.

When I first started teaching, it was for a class someone else had named Composing Your Life Story. I was a published writer by that time; the words "memoir" and "autobiography" were in my personal lexicon, but "life story" was new to me. It sounded a little vague and unprofessional. It sounded like something anyone could do, which is precisely why I now prefer that term over all the others to describe what I teach and practice.

I write my life stories. You write your life stories. We're life story writers. That's what we're doing.

Following are alternative terms for life story writing, with some examples. Note that all definitions are mine, to be taken as guidelines, not word of law.

========================

AUTOBIOGRAPHY. The chronological telling of one's own life from birth to present.

Becoming, BY MICHELLE OBAMA
I often cite this book as a good example of how to write lovingly about a difficult family member without letting that family member off the hook. Michelle Obama's grandfather was a dark cloud of a man, and she displays deft skill in explaining not just how, but why.

MEMOIR. Similar to autobiography, but often just a portion of one's own life, and often more theme-driven than strictly chronological.

Educated, BY TARA WESTOVER
The author tells select stories from her life to advance a thematic narrative that centers broadly on education: how she received schooling exclusively from her parents until she was seventeen, and how she stepped outside the values of her insular family as an adult to pursue an academic and worldly life.

Recipe-driven memoir.
Cooking for Mr. Latte, BY AMANDA HESSER
Ruth Reichl is widely acknowledged as the maestro of the recipe-driven memoir, but I enjoyed reading and still cook from Hesser's 2004 contribution to the genre, a collection of essays and recipes in which she details the beginnings of her relationship with the culinarily challenged man who became her husband. It's a junk-food read, like *Sex and the City* for food nerds and bookworms.

Travel-driven memoir.

The Snow Leopard, BY PETER MATTHIESSEN

Many travel memoirs have followed *The Snow Leopard*, originally published in 1978, but this one is special to me because I read it before I'd traveled much, and definitely before I'd traveled internationally. It's also the first nonfiction book I can remember reading that transported me to a place (specifically the Himalayas) that broadened my ideas of what was possible.

Graphic memoir.

Can't We Talk about Something More Pleasant?, BY ROZ CHAST

If you're a visual artist, you might find that drawings, paintings, or other visual art forms are integral to telling your life story. That was the case for cartoonist Roz Chast when she sat down to tell the story of her aging parents' final years.

Letter-driven memoir.

The Hardest Year: A Love Story in Letters During the Vietnam War, BY CAROLE AND WILLIAM WAGENER

The author, an editing client and former student of mine, structured this memoir around letters she and her husband wrote to each other during the first year of their marriage, when William was serving in Vietnam. Letters are treasures for memoirists. They reveal forgotten facts and emotions, and if they're dated they can also help reconstruct a timeline of events.

Poetic memoir.

Brown Girl Dreaming, BY JAQUELINE WOODSON

This is a memoir in verse, a long prose poem, about an African American girl's upbringing in the 1960s in South Carolina and New York City. It's a story about race, about family, about the differences between the North and the South, and about Woodson's growing into her writer's voice. It's a book geared toward older children and young adults, but the themes transcend age.

Fictional memoir. I once met a man at a book festival who said he was working on a fictional memoir. "Is that a real genre?" he asked. I wasn't sure until I consulted Goodreads and learned it's not only an established genre—Ernest Hemingway wrote a fictional memoir. Hemingway's posthumously published *True at First Light: A Fictional Memoir* is a partly fictionalized account of his final African safari. Given the fickle nature of memory, you could argue that all memoirs are partly fictionalized, but authors who write in this genre do it on purpose.

Other memoir types: **spiritual, inspirational, health, business** . . . and many more.

PERSONAL ESSAY. Plenty of sources educate writers about the dos and don'ts of personal essay writing, but in terms of life story writing a personal essay is any story told from one's life that rallies around a point—a moral, an opinion, a piece of advice, an observation on humanity, or the like. The difference between a story about a memory and a personal essay is that the essay contains an editorial element, something like the difference between a straight news story and an op-ed. The humorist David Sedaris is a great person to study if you're drawn to the essay genre.

ETHICAL WILL. A financial planner with a holistic philosophy was the first person to introduce me to the concept of ethical wills. Imagine a written bequest rather than a material one, a document wherein the writer uses story as a vessel for handing down personal values and advice to future generations.

LIFE REVIEW. We talked a lot about the value of life review when I was a hospice volunteer. Ideally, we would meet patients while they were still capable of holding conversation and willing to review the events of their lives because, we were told, it could bring them peace before they died. We weren't given a template for this life review work, but I've since found that Stanford Medicine has one. In that organization's view, forgiveness—asking for it, and granting it—is an important aspect of life review. The actress Jane Fonda has spoken widely about how conducting a life review when she turned sixty was healing for her.

FAMILY BIOGRAPHY/MEMOIR. Not a genre you'll find labeled in a bookstore, this is what I call projects that delve into the nonfiction stories not only of a single person but of an entire family. The author may still use first person point of view to nice effect, placing themselves in the story as both researcher and protagonist. The best examples I've read of family biography/memoir have been written for individual, not commercial, purposes.

PATCHWORK STORYTELLING.

Why Fathers Cry at Night: A Memoir in Love Poems, Recipes, Love Letters, and Remembrances, BY KWAME ALEXANDER

The Office BFFs: Tales of The Office from Two Best Friends Who Were There, BY JENNA FISCHER AND ANGELA KINSEY

This is perhaps my favorite format of life story writing, knitted together bits and pieces of a life that tell the larger story. A poem here, a recipe there, anecdotes in-between. Photographs or scans of Post-it notes, emails, social media posts, snapshots, ticket stubs, and other ephemera and collectibles. Our lives are messy and scattershot— why shouldn't the presentation of our stories reflect that?

JOURNAL OR DIARY. Journaling and diary-keeping probably need no explanation. If you're looking for a new approach, and if you aren't already familiar with Julia Cameron's prescription for "morning pages" as a means of journaling and exorcizing brain clutter, get yourself a copy of *The Artist's Way* stat.

Who's Your Audience?

Who is your intended audience—your ideal reader—for the memories you're putting on the page?

You may have an audience of one (yourself), of many (everyone/posterity), or of a few (your loved ones). Your audience may change over time, and it may change story to story. Whomever your intended reader might be, it's a good idea to keep them in mind as you write. Not only will keeping your intended audience in mind benefit the reader; it will also make your job easier. Our life stories could be told in multiple ways, leaning on certain details here while omitting information there. Keeping your intended audience in mind will help you decide which way is the correct way to tell the story this time.

I'll give you a silly, four-sentence example using the first time my husband and I ever kissed. Both versions are more or less true. Here's how I would describe the moment to our son (who was twelve years old when I first wrote this):

> *We were riding down an escalator outside the Luxor Hotel in Las Vegas, talking and laughing, when our eyes locked. We'd been friends for years, but suddenly it was clear to both of us that we wanted more. We leaned in at the same time. It's a Hollywood cliché to imagine fireworks blasting off during an epic kiss, but that's exactly what the moment looks like in my mind's eye.*

And here's how I would describe it in a letter to a close girlfriend (and now, you):

> *We'd been carousing in Las Vegas with a group of friends when suddenly we found ourselves on an escalator we didn't recognize, alone and tipsy. I don't know whether we meant to kiss or just bumped into each other while laughing, but once our lips met, we went with it. Someone yelled the oldie but goodie, "Get a room!" And we did.*

There's no crime in writing your stories without considering your audience. If your stories are flowing, don't dam that river by overthinking anything, including audience. But if you're unsure in your storytelling or experiencing whatever writer's block feels like for you, focusing on your intended audience is almost certain to help. When you're feeling stuck, try asking yourself this two-part question, which helps narrow in on audience:

Who am I writing for, and what do I want them to know?

Chances are, answering both parts of that question will reconnect you with the life story you're trying to tell. It's basic advice but easy to forget, even for writers who've been at the craft for a long time. You wouldn't be crazy to transcribe that question—or your own version of it—to a sticky note to look at each time you sit down to write.

———

Before we move on from audience, I want to grant you formal permission to write your life stories for an audience of you and you alone. Why would we write for an audience of *moi*? I know of two good reasons.

First, processing our lives through story can have enormous mental health benefits regardless of who else reads them. (For more on that topic, revisit this book's introduction.)

Secondly, writing with only ourselves in mind helps eliminate self-conscious thought, which thereby illuminates the truth. When students struggle to get to the heart of a story, I often suggest writing it down first as a journal entry no one else will see. Try it. You can return to the story later to soften the edges of raw truth for your future readers if you wish. There's always a risk someone will find your journal, so take appropriate measures to keep it private, and dispose of an only-for-you journal when you no longer need it. In addition, I advise against backing up truly sensitive material to the digital cloud, because you never know. Storage sites could fall victim to hackers or be otherwise compromised. Better to back up your digital files to a personal external hard drive.

Getting Organized

The following are ideas for organizing your thoughts and your storytelling. Don't overwhelm yourself by engaging with each idea; perhaps one or two will resonate with you. I do encourage everyone to consider making at least a rudimentary life timeline. It's that valuable.

TIMELINES. "I started making a timeline, and it got real ugly real fast," said Malinda, one of my editing clients, as she held up an impressively detailed life timeline she'd drawn on a piece of trifold cardboard. Yes, her timeline was jam-packed with handwritten information, and no, it wouldn't translate easily to a digital format, but the timeline was, I countered, gorgeous. Moreover, it served her well as she parsed how to write and organize her stories.

Malinda did on her own what I commonly ask of other editing clients, who are universally surprised when I request a timeline before I begin editing their memoir manuscript.

"Why do I need a timeline when I've already written my story?" they ask.

"Because if you don't know what happened when, you can't expect the reader—or me, your editor—to follow you on your life's journey," I answer.

With a timeline as reference, you won't get lost in your own life, which can easily happen when you're sifting through memories accrued over many decades. Timelines can additionally help you recognize eras of your life that were particularly hectic, peaceful, full of change or challenges, etc. Timelines put your internal calendar on the page, and externalizing all that data makes space for the creative mind to expand. Don't fret if you can't remember exact dates. Even establishing the order in which the events of your life took place will help your storytelling.

The appearance or format of your timeline doesn't matter. Give it whatever form makes sense to you. It doesn't even need to be readable to anyone else. Malinda's timeline, mentioned previously, was horizontal and handwritten, thus the trifold board. Perhaps it's all the word processing I do, but I "drew" my life timeline vertically on the computer as more of a list. It's not viewable on the screen all at once, but my logical brain likes to work with it in that format.

FAMILY TREES. I'm lucky to have had a few genealogy buffs and family historians on my paternal side who did the family tree work for me, but my maternal side doesn't have such enthusiastic documentarians. I only recently began sketching a family tree of that side, after my life story writing revealed how little I knew about my ancestors. I knew that my paternal grandfather, who died when my mother was a child, had been a drinker, a topic I wanted to explore, but I didn't even know his full name, and certainly not the names of his parents or grandparents. That gap in knowledge became a huge writing distraction for me.

My mother's two sisters are still alive, and they helped me fill out the branches of our family tree. I feel more grounded in history and facts now that I have their input, which is creatively liberating. Another bonus of that effort: conversations with my aunts generated new family stories. It cannot be overstated how important it is to ask our elders questions while they're still alive. Not only do their life stories deserve to be heard; their stories hold the answers to questions about our own lives that may one day be too late to ask.

I didn't use fancy software or a template when I made my maternal family tree, though family tree software and templates are just a web search away.

IDENTIFY THEMES. Here I propose two possible methods for identifying your life's themes and generating story ideas. An added benefit of the first exercise is that it tricks you into beginning to write. The product of this exercise is a list, and I firmly believe list-making counts as writing.

Year + Word. Jot down one-word associations for every year of your life. Approach this list with some flexibility. If just one word per year doesn't work for you, allow phrases or even sentences. If one word for every year is daunting, you may bundle years.

When I did my Year + Word list, I didn't burden myself with creativity. My aim was to capture either the first word or name that came to mind for a given year, or a word that expressed the gestalt or general feeling of a year. I allowed myself plenty of time for remembering, but I didn't over-ponder the words.

For an example of how this can work, here's what my first seven years looked like when I did this exercise a few years ago:

Year 1	absence and abundance
Years 2-3	Charles Street
Years 4-5	lilacs
Year 6	princess dress
Year 7	Gary C. and hard orange carpet

"Absence" popped immediately to mind for Year 1. I'd always been told my dad left for National Guard service soon after I was born, but it still surprised me that "absence" was so, well, present for me. It further surprised me when "absence" felt like the most fitting word for five more of my years later down the timeline.

A repeated word or phrase during this exercise constitutes a life theme. I never would have claimed absence as one of my life's themes prior to completing my Year + Word list. Afterward, however, it was so clear. That word had been perched on the lip of my consciousness for decades, just waiting to spring into action. Now, my internal life story writer gets to decide what to do with it, just as you will decide what to do with whatever your own Year + Word list reveals.

Focal Point. One of my students, Anne Brazil, wrote what she calls a "historical memoir" titled *My Dirty Dozen*, which she structured around the stories of twelve of her relatives. Another student is devoting each chapter of her memoir to a different sibling. Yet another student, whose family moved frequently, is organizing her early life stories around the homes her family inhabited.

You could pick almost anything as the organizational focal point of your stories: vehicles you or your family owned, meaningful songs or albums, vacations, holidays, sporting events, your religious arc—you know best what your focal point could be.

Researching the Stories of Your Life

Most of the time, life story writers are themselves the protagonists, or main characters, in their stories. (There are exceptions—family memoirs have a wider cast of main characters, for example.) Our own memories, then, are our greatest research tools. But we can't always count on our memories to fill in all the details, and sometimes we want to include information in our stories that's new even to us. Following are some research avenues that have helped students, clients, and me in the past.

If there's a research method or tool that has helped you, I'd love to add it to the list! Email me at hello@sararoahen.com.

THE LIFE STORY WRITER'S RESEARCH ASSISTANTS

The online resources listed below were accurate as of April 2024.

MEDICAL RECORDS. Ideally, you or the person you're researching will have requested the records before it was too late and stashed them on a hard drive or in a filing cabinet. If you're looking for records from clinics or hospitals and it has been more than ten years, you're probably out of luck. But laws vary by state, and processes vary by institution, so it never hurts to ask. One author I know was able to get some of her records from a hospitalization thirty years prior.

CENSUS RECORDS. From the National Archives website: "The National Archives has the census schedules available from 1790 to 1950, and most have now been digitized by our digitization partners. Family researchers generally find it most helpful to begin with the most current census and work backwards as a strategy for locating people in earlier generations." Some records are only accessible through National Archive and Records Administration (NARA) computers. Visit www.archives.gov/research/census to begin searching and see what's possible.

VETERANS SERVICE RECORDS. Not all military records are available online, but the National Archives offers lots of advice for where to look for what, including photo archives. Visit www.archives.gov/veterans

OTHER RECORDS FROM THE NATIONAL ARCHIVES. It would take a person days to exhaust the possibilities of this website. Visit www.archives.gov/ research for a treasure trove of information.

FAMILYSEARCH.ORG. This is a free service for researching ancestry and making family trees. It's a wonderful resource provided by The Church of Jesus Christ of Latter-day Saints, and I've found valuable information through it. That said, it lists one of my living uncles as deceased (sorry, Tio Danny!). Use it as a tool, not the final word.

ANCESTRY.COM. Another service founded by folks affiliated with The Church of Jesus Christ of Latter-day Saints, Ancestry.com is a for-profit entity. You pay for the service. I haven't personally taken that leap, but I know students, clients, and family members who have benefitted from the investment.

GENEANET.ORG. Yet another site for conducting genealogical research. One student used it to trace her French heritage, and others have confirmed it's a good site for researching European roots. I'm intrigued by the site's call for cemetery and war memorial photographs. What a meaningful way for lay genealogists to get involved. Furthermore, there's an archive of old postcards you can contribute to or search—a new way (to me) of conducting ancestral research.

FINDAGRAVE.COM. A student who has a healthy obsession with cemeteries turned me on to this one. She uses it all the time in researching her family history and says she has located obituaries of distant relatives on the site that have helped bolster her other research findings.

LEGACY.COM. An obituary archive, for searching and submitting. Obituaries frequently contain useful information beyond birth and death dates and can therefore be great resources for life story research. Do bear in mind, though, that obituaries aren't fact-checked. It's easy to get dates, place names, and spellings wrong when you're rushed and grieving.

LIBRARIES. I'm sure it comes as no surprise to read that libraries are prime places for life story research. Never underestimate what our local libraries offer. For example, my local library system grants cardholders access to local and national newspapers; a library edition of Ancestry.com; a library edition of MyHeritage.com, a genealogy database; and HeritageHub, a collection of obituaries and death notices from newspapers across the United States, including some photographs. And that's not to mention the on-site references, like the Local History Collection. Most importantly, remember the librarians, who are there to help at every library.

LIBRARY OF CONGRESS. Speaking of librarians, you may "Ask a Librarian" at the Library of Congress a question about local history or genealogy. The website promises someone will get back to you within five business days.

PHONE BOOKS. Phone books are difficult to find these days, but some may still be warehoused on local library shelves. Or check out the Library of Congress's digitized US Telephone Directory Collection.

GOOGLE EARTH AND GOOGLE MAPS. Invaluable tools for researching former homes and other significant addresses. Google's knowledge of our lives may have a certain creepiness factor, but the ability to pull up a current photo of a former home halfway across the country (or across the world, as my editor, a native of Zimbabwe, pointed out) is a life story writer's dream. My sister, dad, and I noticed that the trees in the front yard of the last house we lived in together could use a trim.

YOUR HOMETOWN MUSEUM (OR YOUR ANCESTOR'S HOMETOWN MUSEUM). I tested this one out by calling the Hoard Historical Museum in my hometown of Fort Atkinson, Wisconsin, to ask for help in locating information about my paternal grandfather, who had some dairy industry patents. The woman who answered the phone offered the email of someone she thought could help me. Before we hung up, she told me to call back if her lead didn't pan out—she'll find a museum staff member to help me research further. It's that simple! Like librarians, museum workers are fairy godparents of the life story writer.

YOUTUBE.COM. I'm forever telling my son you can't find everything on the internet, which is true, and yet YouTube contains almost everything. Archival footage from television and movies, musical performances, books, a channel called Genealogy TV, etc., etc., etc. If you want it, search for it. You never know.

YOUR OWN DIARIES, JOURNALS, CALENDARS, AND OLD ADDRESS BOOKS. Oh, how I wish I'd saved all my old address books. Photographs, letters, emails, and social media posts can be research goldmines too.

How can you tell when it's time to stop researching?

Especially in our digital era, research will take as much time as you give it. And it will keep taking, so at a certain point you need to stop researching and write. Where's that point? It varies person to person, project to project. But if we're honest with ourselves, we'll feel when enough is enough, when our research is serving more as a procrastination device than a means to storytelling.

I have an editing client who's a visual artist. One day, we were talking about the difference between taking a break from an artistic endeavor to fill back up and taking a break from an artistic endeavor out of fear or procrastination. The difference for her is that the former feels good, while the latter feels bad. Research is like that for me: it feels fun and motivating when it's necessary research, and it feels laborious and vaguely nauseating when I'm using research as a means of avoidance.

If you're struggling to decide whether you've researched enough, try putting the research away for a while and seeing where your writing takes you. If it takes you to a problem you can't solve without more research, then you'll know you aren't done.

Honesty vs. Fact

"Memory is not so much a camera as a filter. The particles it holds on to are nothing compared to what leaks through."

John Green, *The Anthropocene Reviewed*

In the summer of 2021, I successfully coaxed my husband and son to take a monthlong road trip from our current home in California to my birth state of Wisconsin, and back. I charted our return route to hit all the landmarks and highlights of the American West I remember visiting on road trips during my youth—The Corn Palace, Badlands National Park, Wall Drug, Mount Rushmore, the Teton Range, moose, red rocks, basic hotels, junk food for breakfast. My dad agreed to join us for a portion of the drive back to California; reliving some of those old memories with three generations in the car would be such a gift.

I've been at this life story writing business long enough to know and expect the limitations of memory. It nevertheless floored me when one stop on our trip revealed just how independently my memory exists from the memories of my own family members. Sometimes my memory even seems to exist independent of fact.

We hadn't planned to stop at the Spam Museum in Austin, Minnesota, but when you're barreling westward along I-90 and your kid sees a billboard and says something like, "What's a spam museum?" from the backseat, you realize you have an obligation to correct a lapse in parenting. While my son measured how tall he was in Spam cans (19.5) and timed himself packaging Spam on a mock assembly line, my dad and I wandered the museum's exhibits and exchanged Spam memories.

"Remember that Spam casserole Mom used to make?" I asked, expecting he would join me in a good chuckle.

"Your mom never made Spam casserole," Dad said.

"Yes, she did. It had sauerkraut in it, and cheese."

"I would remember a Spam casserole. Are you sure you aren't thinking about Reuben casserole? She made that one with canned corned beef."

I called my sister as soon as we left the museum. She laughed. We never ate Spam, she said. Then, it hit me. In all the recipe books and files of my mom's I pored over after she died, I never did find a recipe for Spam casserole. But I'd told the Spam casserole story countless times. I frequently pulled out that detail in conversation to illustrate my 1970s-in-the-Midwest upbringing. Spam casserole was one of the ways I described my warm, cozy, not-much-money but lots-of-love early childhood to myself: my parents were so young and strapped financially with two young kids that Spam casserole was a delicacy. I don't remember loving Spam casserole, but I sure had built an identity around it.

And now it was looking like I may have . . . not made it up exactly, but perhaps conflated two memories? Maybe I'd seen my mom clip a recipe out of the newspaper for Spam casserole. Maybe she'd even bought a can of Spam but then got voted down. Maybe I'd heard about another family eating Spam casserole and stored that piece of information away in my long-term memory, where it had mistakenly gotten filed in the area labeled Things That Actually Happened.

It doesn't really matter. I mean, it's Spam casserole. But I'm telling you this story because I think it's useful for life story writers to recognize the powers and the limitations of memory. If my son had never seen that Spam Museum billboard, or if my dad hadn't been road tripping with us, I'd likely instead be telling you a story about how I grew up eating Spam casserole on the regular. And we'd both believe it.

Would that make it true?

Even now, do you believe my mom made Spam casserole? Do I believe she did? That's a tough one. I've lived that truth all these years, and I've been honest about it. In life story writing, honesty is sometimes different from fact. Our life stories can be honest without always holding up to a strict fact-check. Best to get comfortable with that notion.

It caused me no emotional damage to realize my memories of Spam casserole were questionable or even false. Nor did my questionable memories offend anyone else. Navigating the weaknesses of memory can get trickier than this low-stakes example, but you get the point. Memory is an interpretation of facts, not a mimeograph of them. The subjectivity, pliability, and selectivity of memory are part of what makes life story writing such an interesting endeavor.

My advice for your writing going forward is to honor the truth of your own memories while also remaining curious about them. Maintain a sense of wonder as you recall the events of your past. Are your stories even worth writing if your brain is an unreliable warehouse for what actually happened? Of course they are. Stick to the facts where you can, but don't let an unreasonable attachment to facts hold you back from writing what you honestly remember. If while writing your stories you encounter a discrepancy between your memory and someone else's, you may decide to incorporate their side of the story into your writing, or you may instead decide to lean only into yours.

You get to claim your memories. These are your stories. Your job is not to write them as factually as you can, but as honestly as you can.

Thoughts on Format and Length

The tips and writing prompts in this primer generally aim at narrative writing, meaning I'm trying to help you put one sentence in front of another until you have a collection of stories that can stand on their own. But there are myriad ways to vary the format of your stories. Writers find the most true-to-themselves ways of documenting their lives, and every semester my life story writing students open my eyes to original interpretations of the genre.

Let's look at three of the most common formats life stories tend to take.

ESSAYS. While it may make people who detested high school English classes uneasy, lots of life story writing does naturally read like essay writing (perhaps precisely because the essay was so effectively drilled into us in high school). By definition, an essay is a piece of nonfiction writing that presents an author's personal ideas or beliefs and uses evidence to convince the reader of the author's perspective. Likewise, the author of a piece of life story writing is saying, *Here's what happened in my past, and here are the memories that support my perspective.* No wonder life story writing so frequently takes essay form.

Don't get hung up on whether your life stories are essays, but if you feel like they are, then they probably are.

ANECDOTES AND VIGNETTES. All life stories that stick with us are worth documenting, even the ones that don't seem to have a purpose—no strong moral, no connection to other stories, no wow factor. Six-year-old you happily working for hours one sunny afternoon on a dandelion necklace. Your grandson reaching for his first Cheerio. A day when wearing a particular item of clothing made you feel invincible (in my case, it was a dark avocado Garanimals® ensemble). A family mealtime you'll always remember but don't quite know why.

Anecdotes and vignettes are little autobiographical gems. Don't worry if they're short. Don't worry if they don't have a beginning, middle, and end. Placed between your longer stories, they'll sparkle and provide some variety. And if your life stories are all anecdotes and vignettes, that's perfect. Think of them as a collection of shimmering asides. Professional memoirists publish entire books of anecdotes; the narrative thread between them is that they've all been written by the same person, and that's enough.

Are you an anecdote or vignette writer who wonders,

Are these legitimate stories? Will anyone care about my disjointed memories? If so, adjust your thought process. Instead, ask yourself what you wouldn't give to read a collection of anecdotes written by a loved one who passed away without leaving any written stories behind. There's your answer.

CHAPTERS. If you're working on a book and thinking about your individual writings as chapters, my thoughts on essays and anecdotes still apply. In some memoirs, each chapter is an essay; in other memoirs, some chapters are anecdotes. You have the freedom as the author to decide what constitutes a chapter in your own book. If that's too loosey-goosey for you, if you need a template for what form your chapters ought to take, my best advice is to read enough memoirs to find a few you like. Then, model your approach to your memoir on what the authors of the memoirs you admire have done.

A little more direction on length . . . If the idea of infinite possibilities frustrates you, if you're someone who needs an assignment, I get that. I spent many years trying to figure out how to get words on the page before my first paid writing gig provided the structure I needed to find my footing. My assignment back then was to write an 850-word restaurant review column. Print newspapers are space-restricted; there was no wiggle room. Some weeks I had a lot more than 850 words to say about a given restaurant, and some weeks I struggled to fill the space. But 850 words was my job, and I quickly discovered freedom in the assignment's consistency. I never had to think about the length of the story, I just needed the story to fit the space, and those boundaries were key to my finally getting words on the page. The more words I put on the page, the more confident I became that those words would keep coming.

My greatest wish for you is that this primer will ignite a creative spark toward writing your life stories that nothing could extinguish. I hope you will feel the freedom to get those stories down in your own unique way. But if you're new at this and you're sitting there, pen in hand or fingertips hovering above the keyboard, wishing someone would give you a set of rules, some boundaries, an assignment to help you focus, well then, here it is:

> **Set yourself a weekly word count or page count, and aim for that target. If you try 850 words (roughly two pages) for a while and struggle to get there, drop your goal to 500 words (one page). On the other hand, if 850 words feels too constricting, bump it up to 1,200 (three pages). Then, let those fingers fly.**

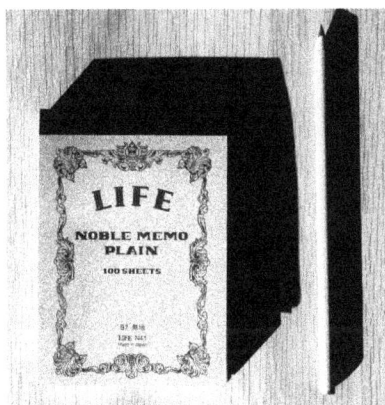

Two Literary Tools

"The first commandment of fiction—Show, Don't Tell— is not part of the memoirist's faith. Memoirists must show and tell."

Patricia Hampl, *I Could Tell You Stories*

I want you to feel comfortable writing your life stories just as they peel off your heart and out of your memory. If you're happy with the first writing of a story, and if writing it came easily to you, then give yourself a cookie from me (preferably chocolate chip) and move on to your next story. This chapter is for those of you who are haunted by writing rules that teachers and bosses may have drilled into you, and for beginning writers who crave the guidance and security rules can provide.

For the haunted and beginning writers, I present two oft-repeated writing precepts—oft-repeated because of their usefulness in getting a clear and engaging story on the page:

- **5 Ws and H (Who, What, When, Where, Why, and How)**
- **Show, Don't Tell**

Journalists and communications majors know the 5 Ws and H rule well. If news reporters and writers of press releases don't ground a story in critical facts in the opening paragraphs, they're likely to lose their readers. Take these first two annotated paragraphs from an article that appeared in *The New York Times* in March 2022:

The Fox News correspondent Benjamin Hall (Who) was injured (What) on Monday (When) in Ukraine (Where) while reporting outside Kyiv (Why—Russia's assault on Ukraine was major news in March 2022, so a newspaper could assume at the time that its readers would understand this Why) and has been hospitalized, the network said.

Executives at Fox News said they had only sparse information about the nature of the journalist's injuries (How—the writer addresses the How by reporting it wasn't yet known How the journalist was injured). Mr. Hall, 39, is a longtime war correspondent who has covered conflicts in Afghanistan, Iraq, Libya, Syria, and other countries. He joined Fox News in 2015 and became a State Department correspondent for the network last year.

See how that works? A hurried newspaper reader can read just the first couple of paragraphs to get the major points of the story; a reader who wants to continue to the end can relax in knowing the basic facts from the start.

Life story writers don't need to cover their 5 Ws and H in the first two paragraphs of a story; our job isn't to inform the train commuter on their way to work about timely happenings. I do, however, believe that stories of any kind are better stories if they cover the 5 Ws and H somewhere. Life story readers, just like newspaper and press release readers, feel confused when *Who, What, When, Where, Why,* or *How* are missing altogether.

If you aren't sure you've covered the 5 Ws and H in one of your stories, read through it and label each one, like how I added labels to the news paragraphs referenced earlier. If you're missing a W or the H, try working it into the story someplace. There will always be a place, even if you need to add another sentence or paragraph. You're likely to find more than one of each W, as our life stories cover a lot more ground than the average news article. That's good; that's strong storytelling.

Sometimes it's difficult to pinpoint the *How* in a story about our past, and that's when calling upon the second storytelling precept, Show, Don't Tell, comes in handy. When fiction and other creative writers are told to Show, Don't Tell, it means that instead of simply stating facts *(this happened, and then this happened, and then this happened)*, they need to pump up their writing with more description, more dialogue, more scene-setting, more sensory details, more character emotions, more similes, more metaphors, more, more, more. In short, when fiction and other creative writers engage in showing rather than telling, that means they use action, images, and emotions, in addition to facts, to help their story unfold.

Showing rather than telling is a valid way to approach life story writing too. If you're someone who likes to incorporate dialogue, scene-setting, sensory details, and lots of description into your writing—maybe even a bunch of similes and metaphors—go for it. Show, Don't Tell to your heart's desire. Don't get hung up on the notion that those bells and whistles are required, though. Because we're writing about ourselves in our life stories, there's an easier, and equally compelling, way for us life story writers to engage in Show, Don't Tell, and it's that H. That *How*.

I offer two ways to tease out the *How* in your life stories. Both go a long way toward showing, not telling, and both help the writer incorporate more emotion into the story:

1. When you write about the past, let your reader know *How* what happened affected your inner life as you were experiencing events back then.

2. Let your reader know *How* what happened back then affects your inner life now. Have your feelings about what happened back then evolved over time? Looking at that time from the perspective of the person you are today, *How* do you feel now about what happened back then?

To give an example of covering the 5 Ws and H in life story writing, as well as incorporating Show, Don't Tell by way of emotional experience, I'm borrowing from one of my life story writing students, Dian De Sha. The following is an excerpt from the beginning of an essay she wrote in March 2022, again when Ukraine was under vicious attack by Russia. I haven't labeled the Ws in her story, but I have highlighted the H.

> *75 Years Under Nuclear Threat*
>
> *I was born in the nuclear age, 81 days after US bombs destroyed Hiroshima, Japan (August 6, 1945, followed three days later by Nagasaki), and one day after the Charter of the United Nations was ratified and the UN was born (October 24, 1945).*
>
> *My first war-related memory is from when I was four, when I was conscripted by my pacifistic, anti-war parents into helping the local American Friends Service Committee pack relief boxes for a post-war-ravaged Germany. I was called on to sacrifice my beloved doll for adoption overseas.*

> *It was painful to do the "right thing" at four, but I vividly remember laying her in the box with sweaters and shoes and blankets, closing the lid, and feeling sad but hopeful that she would be loved in Germany, wherever that was.*

Then, at the end of her essay, Dian provides the reader insight into *How* what she lived through as a child affected her inner life in March 2022, when she wrote the story:

> *Today, as Putin threatens the world with nuclear war and I watch Ukrainians fighting tanks with their bodies, I cry for their struggle, for the injustice of their plight, for their pain and privation. I long to help. And I cannot comprehend that any madman would unleash horror that would eclipse Hiroshima, Chernobyl, and Fukushima, and annihilate the living beings of this world.*

And that's how a life story writer incorporates the 5 Ws and H, using the *How* as an opportunity to explore their own inner life, then and now—which achieves a whole lot of showing, don't you think?

Photos and Memorabilia

Unlike my son, whose every milestone, birthday cake presentation, and otherwise significant life event has been documented on video with his parents' smartphones, I know of just a few videos from my early life—and those videos would take some real effort to dig up and figure out how to watch. Instead, I have albums and boxes filled with snapshots, both staged and candid, taken with handheld film cameras. If your early life predated the digital age, as mine did, you likely have the same.

Photos make fantastic additions to life stories, for at least two reasons:

1. Photos provide the reader an added dimension of entertainment. The image complements your written word and even helps expand the reader's imagination, placing the reader more concretely in the moment in time your story evokes.

(I'm trying not to say a photo is worth a thousand words here, but . . .)

2. Photos help jog the writer's memory.

I recently came across a random photo that brought that second point into stark relief. Here it is:

It's an inconsequential photo in so many ways, one that I may even have erased had it been taken in the digital age because it shows nothing overtly monumental. Just my cousins and me (left), sitting at the kitchen table in the house where my nuclear family lived on the outskirts of town for roughly eight years, from second grade until I was a junior in high school. But I'm so grateful to have it now, as it helped haul many memories from the basement safe of my memory bank. This is what certain holidays looked like, particularly Easter, and I can smell the scalloped potatoes that would have filled one of the casserole dishes on the kitchen counter just beyond where we sit. There's my mom talking on the brown, corded, push-button phone that swallowed so many of my teenage hours (how I loved her in that black dress with the red sash belt!), and beyond her are the dark silhouettes of more guests eating in the dining room. I'd forgotten about that kitchen wallpaper—pears and grapes—and that rainbow devilled egg tray hanging on the side of the cupboards. What kind of soda were we drinking? Oh, remember how our mugs hung from little hooks like that beneath the cupboard (below the deviled egg tray)? Who's the hunky guy in the white jeans? Must've been an exchange student or a boyfriend. I know I would've been tickled to be sitting with my kind, pretty, funny older cousins.

This photo holds stories for me. Your photos hold stories too. Use them. Get them into your larger life story, whether that means using the photos as springboards for stories, or simply digitizing photos that illustrate important milestones, events, and people from your life, and adding captions to them. I have the same advice for ephemera—the ticket stubs (remember those?), business cards, handwritten jottings-down, brochures, newspaper clippings, menus, and other personal collectibles that have been stowed away in the garage or have yellowed with age in a drawer. Excavate them, shine the light of the present on them, and use them to tell your stories. Just like with photographs, the memories will pour out of such mementos.

Once you've written a story or two, you may or may

not decide to keep the mementos. It takes just a piece of tape to incorporate a ticket stub into a story, but you may decide to include only a photo of something more unwieldy, like an oversized menu or a piece of clothing. You may even decide the story is enough, no visual aid necessary. However you incorporate physical memories into your life stories, this exercise provides a grand opportunity for decluttering and getting rid of bits and pieces from the past that no longer serve you in their physical form. In other words, keep the story, trash the thing.

A poem that speaks beautifully to the power of photographs:

Another Life
BY DEBORAH CUMMINS

My mother, 18, the summer before she married,
lounges belly-down in the sun,
books and grass all around, her head on her hands
propped at a jaunty angle.
She smiles in a way I've never seen
at something beyond the camera.
This photograph I come back to again and again
invites me to re-write her life.
I keep resisting, certain
I'd have no part in it, her first born
though not exactly. A boy first,

two months premature, my brother
who lived three days, was buried in a coffin
my father carried. "The size of a shoe box,"
he said, the one time he spoke of it.
And my mother, too, offered only once
that she was pregnant and so they married.
Drawn to this saw-edged snapshot,
I'm almost convinced to put her in art school.
Single, she'd have a job in the city,
wouldn't marry. There'd be no children
if that would make her this happy.
But I'm not that unselfish, or stupid.
And what then, too, of my beloved sister,
her son I adore?
So let me just move her honeymoon
from the Wisconsin Dells to the Caribbean.
Let the occasional vacation in a Saugatuck cabin
be exactly what she wanted. The house
she so loved she won't have to sell.
Winters, there's enough money to pay the bills.
There are no cigarettes, no stroke, no paralysis.
Her right hand lifts a spoon from a bowl
as easily as if it were a sable-hair brush
to an empty canvas.
And the grass that summer day
on the cusp of another life
is thick, newly mown, fragrant.

Assumptions, Making and Avoiding Them

We don't get through this life alone. We do it alongside a cast of supporting characters, which makes it all but impossible to write about our own lives without also writing about other people. Deciding how, and how much, to write about other people can be a tricky endeavor, especially if what we have to say isn't praise. Let's explore one aspect of this dynamic between the life story writer and their cast of characters, namely what happens when we assume what motivated the other people in our stories to do what they did.

My now-husband, Matt, and I arrived in New Orleans in 1999 while still in our twenties. He was entering medical school, and I was a restaurant cook. Alongside the friends and neighbors who we met in that city, we lived through our extended adolescence, career changes, the purchase of our first home, Hurricane Katrina, a miscarriage, career heartbreaks, the birth of our son, the death of three parents, a dozen and a half Mardi Gras seasons, and a gazillion pots of gumbo. When we moved to California in 2016, we left behind a lot of living. I was ready for our move to the West Coast but not exactly cheerful about it.

For our first year in California, at least, I did everything I could to push New Orleans out of my conscious mind. I didn't try to forget the people I cared about there, but I buried our Mardi Gras costume bin and New Orleans cookbooks in the garage and found other ways to shield myself from reminders of our former life.

Matt, on the other hand, began every workday by blasting the Neville Brothers, Galactic, Dr. John, Rebirth Brass Band—the most iconic New Orleans music of our era there—while he whooped and shouted and sang along in the shower. He literally bounced to the kitchen for his coffee. I made space for his joy, but I resented it. I tried not to be a wet blanket, but I'm sure my body language betrayed my thoughts. I perceived Matt's ability to transition from our former full life to this new fragile one without a single hang-up as a clear character flaw.

I wrote the following sentence in a journal I kept during that time:

> *Anyone with a heart could see this is a time for a fugue, not a dance party.*

I guess I'd forgotten how, in New Orleans, they dance at funerals.

One day about five years after our move, I asked Matt the question we often ask each other when the wildfires rage or our California property tax bill comes due: "Do you regret moving to California?" After a long moment of thought, he answered how we always answer: no.

"I was really depressed that first year, though," he said. "I missed our friends and our way of life so much. That's why I was always blasting New Orleans music."

Ooooooooooooooh.

While I'd been vilifying him for what I'd assumed was a lack of feeling, Matt had been experiencing some level of sadness. Of course he had! A major move is hard on everyone for a while, no matter the circumstances. I'd been too mired in my own emotions to recognize the truth of Matt's experience.

I tell this story to illustrate how natural it is to assume we know what motivates the people in our lives to do the things they do. I tell this story to illustrate how often our assumptions are wrong, even about people we've known intimately for decades. If I'd written about this time in our lives at any point during our first five years in California, I would've presented Matt as the unfeeling ogre stomping all over my homesickness with his psychopathic joy. Today, because I no longer assume what motivated him to blast that music, it's a more nuanced story. My experience of Matt's behavior at the time hasn't changed, but the way I tell the story has. The lesson here for the life story writer is simple. When in doubt, don't assume.

What about the times when we can't go back and ask someone about their motivations? Aren't we left with assumptions? Good question. Yes, but it's still possible, and generous, to give the other people in our stories the benefit of the doubt. By which I mean this: if you can't be certain why the other people in your stories did certain things, what motivated them, you can try to avoid assuming the worst.

That doesn't mean you shouldn't be honest about what the people in your stories did. Matt did blast New Orleans music at the very time when it hurt me to hear it, and maybe he could have been more sensitive to my needs. It also doesn't mean you shouldn't be honest about your reaction to whatever they did when you write your stories. I did wonder at the blackness of Matt's heart. But you can write those truths while also remaining curious about—not assuming—what motivated them.

I don't feel badly about trash-talking Matt in my journal. That's what journals are for. But let's say I'd written that story in a more formal way, something for the family record. Here's an example of how I could have extended Matt some benefit of the doubt without letting him off the hook or minimizing my own experience:

Anyone with a heart could see this was a time for a fugue, not a dance party. I felt like I'd married a man with a black heart. Couldn't he see I was suffering? Obviously, we were in different spaces—he was getting ready every morning to show up at a new high-stakes job in a new town, while I hadn't begun to figure out my California identity yet. I waited out our emotional disconnect, not for the first time.

What I'm suggesting is a version of trying to walk in another person's shoes before you put words on the page about them. There's a reward for the life story writer who makes such an effort. Letting go of assumptions isn't only generous to the other people in our stories; it can be freeing for us writers too. It can bring us to a higher level of understanding about the past. You may never know what actually motivated someone else, but opening your mind to the less damning possibilities may soften the edges of resentment and add some sweetener to any bitter memories.

Humans assume. You'll never reach perfection with letting go of assumptions, in life or in life story writing, but your stories—and your experience of them—will be richer if you try.

Emotional Health

In the introduction to this guide, we covered the undeniable benefits of life story writing. But what about when life story writing stirs up tough emotions? It happens, and I know firsthand how challenging it can be to find your way out when you've written yourself into a dark tunnel. The good news: that tunnel has escape hatches.

Of all the brainy quotes and writing maxims, this is the one that resonates loudest with me:

We write to understand.

We write to understand where we came from, we write to understand where we're going. We write to understand the world and the people around us. We write to know the unknowable, to explain the inexplicable. In the words of Flannery O'Connor, or often attributed to her anyway, "I write because I don't know what I think until I read what I say."

Those words are inspiring to me, heartening, and yet it's also true that writing to understand can put a lot of pressure on our writing lives. The truth is, writing about our lives doesn't always feel good, and sometimes the writing doldrums appear unexpectedly, seemingly out of nowhere, which can be confusing. Students have asked me what to do when writing about the tough stuff makes them sad. They ask questions like,

> *How do I write about the darker times of my life without getting sucked into a black hole?*

> *I thought life story writing was supposed to be cathartic. Why does dredging this up get me down?*

> *What am I doing wrong? Should I stop writing?*

I'm not a therapist. I'm a writer. But I'm a writer who has struggled with keeping the words flowing amid my own memory's ups and downs, and I can offer some lessons learned.

JOURNALING. I've had lots of success keeping myself emotionally afloat with journaling in different forms. In recent years I've found that beginning or wrapping up the day with a quick entry in a gratitude journal helps calm my busy mind. I make a list of ten things I'm grateful for. Some are specific to the day (good conversation with a friend), some aren't (the ever-present, bracing scent of eucalyptus from a grove adjacent to our home). On some days it's easier than on others to come up with ten—coffee, our cats, and California weather are always there for me when I come up short. I feel more settled after that bit of writing, and the practice has generated many ideas for future stories.

TRY A DIFFERENT WRITING STYLE. At one point in my writing life, I realized that writing about my own life in the style of memoir was bringing me down. Intuition told me that I should try exploring my life with fiction instead. Did it work? No one would ever publish the novel I wrote, in part because I never finished even a first draft, but the exercise of applying fiction to my story was a success because it jolted me out of my funk and got me excited about writing again. You wouldn't need to do something that drastic, pivoting from memoir to fiction. Several of my life story writing students flow from narrative prose to poetry, and back again. You could even try a change as subtle as shifting point of view, moving from a first person (I) narrator to a third person (she/he/they) narrator, for example. Or writing your stories in letters instead of essays. Or a series of lists. Get creative.

MORNING PAGES. I've done morning pages off and on throughout my adult life. Here's an excerpt from Julia Cameron's book *The Artist's Way* to explain the concept. This is a small part of her explanation of morning pages, but you'll get the idea.

What are morning pages? Put simply, the morning pages are three pages of longhand writing, strictly stream-of-consciousness: "Oh, god, another morning. I have NOTHING to say. I need to wash the curtains. Did I get my laundry yesterday? Blah, blah, blah . . ." They might also, ingloriously, be called brain drain, since that is one of their many functions.

In providing a place for everything, morning pages make me feel lighter every day when I do them. They absorb all the white noise from my subconscious mind, which allows my creativity to flow more freely. True confession: I don't think morning pages need to be done in the morning. That's a morning-person bias. The important thing is doing them, not the time of day.

WHEN POSSIBLE, TAKE AS LONG AS IT TAKES WITH A TOUGH TOPIC. If you want to give your toughest topics their due, let them fully unfurl before boxing them into paragraphs. Take breaks. Turn away briefly from difficult stories when you sense they need to breathe, or tantrum, or rest. Write about something else for a while.

INTENTIONALLY FOCUS ON JOYFUL MEMORIES. When your writing brings you down, or when your main writing topic is overwhelmingly negative and you can't see your way through to the light, try making a list of all the things that have impacted your life positively. Write about those for a while.

ARE YOU WRITING TO THE WRONG AUDIENCE? This happens all the time. Writing to the wrong audience can make us feel disconnected from and uneasy about our writing. Fortunately, there's an easy fix. Maybe the audience you've had in your mind's eye while writing has been your parole officer, when really your intended audience is other wrongly convicted parolees. Or maybe you've had your best friend in mind when it's your kids whose reading experience you care most about. Or you've been writing for your own inner critic, when what would really open your story up is writing letters to your younger self. A little correction of audience is sometimes all it takes to get us back on track and excited about our storytelling again.

SEE A THERAPIST. It can be difficult to parse a creative depression from a clinical depression. And, like I said, writing our life stories can bring a lot of strong feelings to the surface. Sometimes those strong feelings are welcome, and sometimes they're overwhelming. You're not a poor writer or a weak person if you find you can't write your way back to a happy place. If you don't believe me, just ask to see my therapy receipts! On the flip side, one of my students told me that writing his life stories has benefitted his therapy sessions. The process of writing helps him learn more about himself and organize his thoughts before he talks to his therapist. This student also pointed out that writing his life stories has brought more joy than difficult emotions to his life.

DON'T STOP WRITING. Remember, we write to understand. Every time we put words on the page, we come away with a deeper understanding of ourselves and the lives we've lived. While some stories may get heavy, because life is sometimes heavy, the net result of our writing should be feelings of positivity. We're survivors! We've lived a lot of life! We have stories to tell!

Six Writing Prompts to Get You Started

The following writing prompts are designed to invigorate your inner storyteller and help you begin to put your memories on the page. Each prompt contains many sub-prompts, so you may be inspired to write more than six stories or anecdotes. However the stories emerge, whatever form they take on the page—that's the correct way. Don't overanalyze at this juncture. Make getting started your only aim right now.

PROMPT #1: BEGINNINGS. Begin at the beginning by writing about the people who came before you.

You could focus on your faraway ancestors, including some of your genealogy, or keep it chronologically closer with a writing about your grandparents. If you've made a trip to your ancestral homeland, you could make this piece of writing a sort of travelogue.

Some of you might not know anything about your biological ancestors. If that's your truth, tell that story. An absence of information needn't hold you back from writing what you do know, as well as what you wish you knew and the emotional impact of not knowing.

You're writing your life stories, so any information you record about the life you've lived, including emotional reflections, is relevant and important.

This is how the poet Joyce Sutphen writes about the people who came before her:

More of Everything
    BY JOYCE SUTPHEN

The people who made me possible
came from places in middle Europe,
riding steamships through the middle of
the nineteenth century. They didn't
always get their right names, and if
they wrote home, I never heard.

The people who made me possible
worked hard clearing the land, tree
by stump by prairie grass, hauling
rock off the fields and gravel to the
roads. They seldom stopped to consider
if here was better than over there—

wherever that was. If they regretted
anything, they didn't say, and they
didn't tell stories about the old country;
my people didn't make a fuss

about being born or dying early—
they always died early—which

explains why they loved weddings
and christenings, birthdays and
the Fourth of July—any time they could
sit at a picnic table listening to
a polka band, going back many
times for more of everything.

"More of Everything" by Joyce Sutphen from *Carrying Water
to the Field: New and Selected Poems.* © University of Nebraska
Press, 2019. Reprinted with permission of the poet.

Another way of approaching the prompt of "beginnings" is by writing about the people who made you possible, to use the poem's language. If you approach a story from this angle, feel free to interpret the prompt creatively. For example, if the people who literally made you possible—your biological ancestors and family—don't deserve credit for who you are, then write about the people who made you possible in a spiritual sense.

PROMPT #2: CHILDHOOD. Write about a significant event from your childhood.

That one-sentence prompt will either get you straight to work, or it will overwhelm you with possibilities. If you're in the latter, overwhelmed, camp, begin by making a list. On a sheet of real or digital paper, list ten significant childhood memories you regularly return to, either in your mind's eye or in the stories you tell people about yourself. Don't overthink your choices. Go with the first memories that come to you. Do you remember acing or bombing a test at school? Lying to a grown-up? Jumping into a frigid lake? Losing a peer to illness or tragic accident? Catching fireflies? Evacuating for a hurricane or wildfire? Finding stillness in the trees beyond your backyard?

Most people could write infinitely about childhood, and perhaps you will, but you'll never write about it at all if you don't start with the first story. Now's the time for that first story.

Be sure to save that list! You can refer to it when you're ready to document another childhood story, either right away because you're so motivated, or in some future moment of inspiration.

If you need more targeted prompting, explore one of the following ideas:

- Was there a time when your childhood took an unexpected turn, for better or for worse? Did your parents divorce? Did you move? Did you change schools? Did you need to begin working at a young age? Did you win an award?
- Can you recall any particularly joyful events from your childhood—small joy or big joy? Perhaps you got your ears pierced, or celebrated a significant event with extended family, or received a treasured gift.
- What kinds of games did you like to play as a child, either indoor games or outdoor games?

PROMPT #3: PARENTS AND PARENTAL FIGURES. Write about your parents. Include the basics: What were their names? What do you know about where they came from? How did they meet? Also include the subtler and more specific details: What did they look like? What were their struggles and successes? What was/ is the quality of your relationship with them? What was/ is the quality of their relationship with each other? (I use "them" here in a general way—depending upon your upbringing, it may refer to one parent, or four parents, or some other number. Insert your unique circumstances.)

This is the section of your life story where you

might include information about having been adopted or growing up in the foster care system. If you had stepparents or were raised by people other than your biological parents, that could go here too.

Some writers choose to write different sections for each parent/parental figure; other writers weave all parents into one narrative piece of writing. There's no best way of approaching this one. Just get your memories on the page.

Writing about parents can be a tricky business, emotionally speaking. Take good care of yourself if you feel big emotions coming to the surface. Deep breaths. Brisk walks. Loud music. Plenty of chocolate.

PROMPT #4: YOUR GENERATION. Write about your generation.

What makes your generation special?

What do you see as beneficial to having been born into your generation?

What hardships are specific to your generation?

To what changes in cultural or societal norms was your generation asked to adapt?

In what ways do you identify—or not—with the stereotypical profile of your generation?

What do you think are your generation's greatest contributions to the world?

What mistakes or miscalculations do you think your generation will be known for in the future?

Another way of exploring impacts on your generation is by writing about the most significant historical moment you remember. What was it, how did it impact society at large, and how did it affect the way you think about or operate in the world?

PROMPT #5: SCHOOLING. Write about your education.

What schools did you attend? What teachers influenced you the most? What were your favorite and least favorite subjects? Were you more interested in sports, or shop class, or your social life, than in academics? Or did you excel at grade-getting but fumble in other areas?

Were you homeschooled? Unschooled?

Did you leave school early for the workforce?

What about higher education? Did you attend college or technical school? Maybe you spent a year abroad, or studied at seminary, or learned a skill in the military.

You may have no positive memories of your schooldays at all. If that's the case, write about where you did find quality education in your life. Maybe it was at your grandmother's hip in the kitchen. Maybe it was working the family farm. Maybe it was listening to talk radio, or watching television, or hanging out at a library.

PROMPT #6: PETS AND OTHER ANIMALS. Write about the animals in your life, past or present.

You could do this in so many ways. You could write about how your pets came to you; the eras of your life they saw you through; how they were similar to or different from each other; how and when they crossed what pet owners in my social media feed often call "the Rainbow Bridge"; and so forth.

You could insert humor (certainly our pets create lots of blooper moments), you could write a tribute, or you could write from the point of view of a pet. A student once wrote a touching and hilarious essay that revealed what she imagined were her springer spaniel's thoughts throughout the day.

This prompt isn't limited to dogs and cats. Bring on the turtles! The raccoons! The tarantulas!

Some more ideas:

- Are you passionate about animal rescue?
- Does the idea of having a pet turn you off? Why?
- Do you have allergies that prohibit you from getting a furry pet?
- Have you ever had an unusual animal as a pet?
- Some people stock their aquariums with exotic sea life. Is that you?
- Did your parents outlaw pets? If so, how did that affect the choices you made regarding pets in adulthood?
- Has a pet (yours or someone else's) ever ruined an outfit? A piece of furniture? An entire day?
- How have you memorialized your pets when they've passed away?
- Maybe you have a pet-ran-away-but-miraculously-returned story.
- Some animals offer therapeutic benefits. Do you have an emotional support animal, a guide dog, or a dog trained to detect medical problems?

- Have you ever fostered an animal?
- Do you reject the idea of having a pet on moral grounds?
- Has your love for an animal ever changed your dietary decisions?
- If you're a horseback rider, a beekeeper, a caged bird lover, a ferret owner, or the like, be sure to provide details. Less common human-animal relationships offer an opportunity to inform the reader in addition to entertaining them.

Acknowledgments

Big thanks to the life story writing students who have joined my classes since 2018. It's only because of our writing community, and your stories, that I conceived of this primer. Special thanks to Heidi Hathaway, Malinda Lodge, Bob Smith, and Brandon Jones, beta readers extraordinaire.

Thanks to Joanna Klein, whose invitation to join her Journey to Legacy™ writing course helped deepen my knowledge of the benefits of life story writing.

Gratitude to Ilana Singer Rand, my copyeditor, and to Vanessa Salvia and Debbie Hanoch for their keen eyes in proofreading.

I'm so honored to have been given permission to include Deborah Cummins's and Joyce Sutphen's poems. Praise be to the poets!

Kevin Lum and Craig Damrauer: Your sharp observations were invaluable.

Most of all, thanks to my Demitasse Press cofounder, Dorka Hegedus, without whose friendship and collaboration this primer may never have come to fruition, and certainly wouldn't be as handsome.

Notes

James Pennebaker's original research:
J. W. Pennebaker, "Writing About Emotional Experiences as a Therapeutic Process," Psychological Science 8, issue 3 (1997): 162-166.

An interesting reflection on the original research, and subsequent findings:
J. W. Pennebaker, "Expressive Writing in Psychological Science," Perspectives on Psychological Science 13, issue 2 (2018): 226-229.

Bibliography

Alexander, Kwame. *Why Fathers Cry at Night: A Memoir in Love Poems, Recipes, Love Letters, and Remembrances.* New York: Little, Brown & Company, 2023.

Brazil, Anne Jennings. *My Dirty Dozen: 12 Family Heroes.*

Cameron, Julia. *The Artist's Way: A Spiritual Path to Higher Creativity, Tenth Anniversary Edition.* New York; Jeremy P. Tarcher/Penguin, 2002.

Chast, Roz. *Can't We Talk about Something More Pleasant?* New York: Bloomsbury USA, 2016.

Cummins, Deborah. *Counting the Waves.* Word Press, 2006.

Fischer, Jenna, and Angela Kinsey. *The Office BFFs: Tales of the Office from Two Best Friends Who Were There.* New York: Dey Street Books, 2022.

Green, John. *The Anthropocene Reviewed: Essays on a Human-Centered Planet.* New York: Dutton, 2021.

Hampl, Patricia. *I Could Tell You Stories: Sojourns*

in the Land of Memory. New York: W. W. Norton & Company, 1999.

Hemingway, Ernest. *True at First Light: A Fictional Memoir.* New York: Scribner, 2000.

Hesser, Amanda. *Cooking for Mr. Latte.* New York: W. W. Norton & Company, 2003.

Matthiessen, Peter. *The Snow Leopard.* London: Penguin Classics, 2008.

Obama, Michelle. *Becoming.* New York: Crown, 2018.

Sutphen, Joyce. *Carrying Water to the Field: New and Selected Poems.* Lincoln: University of Nebraska Press: 2019.

Wagener, Carole, and William Wagener. *The Hardest Year: A Love Story in Letters During the Vietnam War.* Carole and William Wagener, 2023.

Westover, Tara. *Educated: A Memoir.* New York: Random House, 2018.

Woodson, Jaqueline. *Brown Girl Dreaming.* New York: Nancy Paulson Books, 2016

Zinsser, William. *On Writing Well: The Classic Guide to Writing Nonfiction, 30th Anniversary Edition.* New York: HarperCollins, 2006.

Index

About the Author

Sara Roahen is the author of *Gumbo Tales: Finding My Place at the New Orleans Table*, and the co-editor of *The Southern Foodways Alliance Community Cookbook*. Her writing has appeared in many online and print publications, including the *Los Angeles Times, Bon Appétit, Tin House, and Oxford American*. A writer, editor, coach, and teacher living in California, Roahen is a cofounder of Demitasse Press.

www.sararoahen.com

If you're hungry for more, please look for our next book, *A Year of Tips and Prompts for Memoir and Life Story Writers: Putting More Memories on the Page*, soon to be published by Demitasse Press.